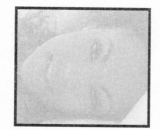

Foolish/Unfoolish

REFLECTIONS ON LOVE

Ashanti

HYPERION NEW YORK

This book is dedicated to my grandparents, Yvonne Myers and Jimmy Davis

I want to say thank you to all of my family and friends for their support, and to Uncle Curt (they left you out on the album!). Thank you to my fabulous team, the untouchables; to Steph for getting this deal; to Veronica, Jerry, Linda, Kendal, and Rich; to Gotti and Ja and my entire Murder Inc. family—DEF JAM, AJM, and the Baeza family; to my travel party family—Shereese, Jeff, Rick, and Lyfe; to Hyperion; and especially to all the fans who support and keep Ashanti hot. And of course to God for keeping us all here and giving us all the strength to face another day.

Library of Congress Cataloging-in-Publication Data

Ashanti.
    Foolish/unfoolish : reflections on love / by Ashanti.—
1st ed.
      p. cm.
    ISBN 1-4013-0030-8
    1. Love poetry, American.   2. Poets, American—
21st century—Biography.   3. Women singers—
United States—Biography.   4. Ashanti.   I. Title.

PS3601.S27 F66   2002
782.421643'0268—dc21   2002032866

Hyperion books are available for special promotions and premiums. For details contact Hyperion Special Markets, 77 West 66th Street, 11th Floor, New York, New York, 10023-6298, or call 212-456-0100.

Book design by Lisa Stokes

FIRST EDITION

10 9 8 7 6 5 4 3 2 1

Foolish/Unfoolish

Introduction

I've always written poetry and reflections in my journal, but I never thought I'd collect them in a book. These writings were just a way for me to take things that happened in my life and remember them later on. Sometimes I'd use these poems as lyrics in later songs, and sometimes they'd just stay poetry or journal entries. I've been writing this way since I was thirteen years old! Early in high school, I was placed in honors English, where I understood all the fancy-schmancy poets and I was able to explain them to the teacher and the class. Later on, outside of the textbooks and the studying, I'd come up with an idea at a club or in the car waiting for a friend and as soon as I'd get home I'd write it in my book as poetry. Usually I would write about love and relationships. Sometimes the poetry would be silly—but you often sound silly when you're talking about love.

There's really only one thing that made me want to publish a book of my writings—my fans! I receive so many letters from fans saying they were inspired by this song or that song. Since most of my songs are about love, too, I get lots of letters asking advice about relationships, or telling me they used to be "foolish" and now they're "unfoolish" in love as a result of listening to my lyrics. I am so pleased and grateful that my ideas about love have had such a positive effect on people. Because of those letters from fans (and face-to-face meetings with fans!), I decided to collect some of my writing in this book.

So, here you'll find many of my ideas, musings, poetry, and reflections about love, as well as stories of the actual events that moved me to write some of the pieces. I hope you enjoy them, and I hope that they'll inspire and encourage you to express yourself. Don't belittle or neglect your own thoughts about life!

FALLING

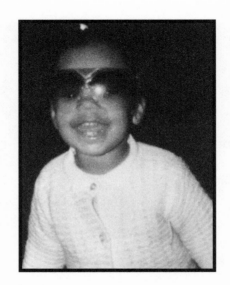

I used to do lots of crazy things for love.

I would leave my house late in the middle of the night—at two, three, five in the morning! I'd drive out to my boyfriend's or drive to the city to pick him up from his job. Sometimes I would go to the train station, where I would sit in the car for thirty minutes or an hour waiting for the train to come. If he missed his stop, I would have to drive and follow the train and try to find the next stop.

I had moved to Atlanta for a little while and it was really, really hard. It was very hard for the relationship. But when you're in love, you try to make it work. I was definitely in love. And I really didn't want to move. I was having a good time, and I found someone who I was head-over-heels for. When I moved it really hurt, but we kept it going. I would call every day, and we would speak on the phone for hours! My boyfriend and I would do things like look at the clock and match up the time. He would dial at an exact minute and I would pick up the phone so it didn't ring at three in the morning. I was living with my uncle in Atlanta, and he really didn't want to hear the phone ringing that late. I would also fly into New York without telling my parents that I was coming and I would stay with my boyfriend for three days or something. I would call them from a pay phone, pretending that I was in Atlanta! But I was really staying at his house. Then I'd tell them that I was coming home in a couple of days, but I was actually already in New York.

You Always Make Me Feel

You always seem to make me feel
that this love is real

You're on my mind
And I know that you are
by my side

I want to let you know
that I'm so in love
with you

The way you treat me
takes me to another place
I want to wrap my arms around you
and gently kiss your face

I'll tell you once again, boy
I'll share your love, sorrow, and joy
I want to spend time
with my baby

When I look into your eyes
I still get butterflies
I know this love will grow
That's why I'm letting you know
Baby, you always seem to make me feel
that this love is real

When I wrote "You Always Make Me Feel" I was in a relationship with this guy and I really didn't have to worry about this whole trust thing. I felt that everything was going really well in the relationship, and that he really, honestly cared about me a lot. I knew he would never intentionally try to hurt me. I didn't have to worry about the whole cheating thing. I knew in my heart that everything was all gravy. It made me feel good to be around someone who could make me laugh and make me smile, and not have to worry about him being out with other girls and me being caught with egg on my face. It was a brand-new relationship but it was still very strong.

One of the best dates I ever had was at T.G.I. Friday's.

I remember just looking into his eyes and just talking, and having so much in common and laughing and having a great time. That was one of the first times I felt really, really connected with him. It wasn't anything spectacular, crazy, or romantic—it was just romantic in the way that I was happy because we were really connecting so early in the relationship. I just remember being at Friday's and not really even seeing anyone else around, because I was so into this guy and our conversation. And I knew he felt the same way. I remember ordering chicken fingers and ice cream— we had so much food at our table because we were just talking and eating and enjoying each other's company. And I knew my mom was going to try to make me come home fairly early. I didn't have a curfew, but she wanted me to be home. So we ordered so much food just to stay as long as possible. When we finally got up to leave, we kissed in the restaurant—almost forgetting that so many people were around! That was our first public kiss. We had a lot of nice dates, but that one sticks out.

 Imagine

Every morning I am thanking my stars
Feel so lucky having you in my arms
Wouldn't be the same without you, babe
There's not a thing about you I would change
I'm incomplete when you're far away
And when you're here, you make me whole again
At first I really didn't trust it or believe it
I found someone who will make me say this and mean it

Couldn't imagine life without you
I want to wrap my arms around you
You're like a miracle in the month of May
I just want to kiss your face

Sometimes I have to stop and stare
Might even run my fingers through your hair
Just to see that this is not a dream
I've got to see you smiling back at me
And I'm okay as long as you're okay
Don't have to ask, I know you feel the same
At first I really didn't trust it or believe it
I found someone who could make me say this and mean it

My ex and I were coming back from the movies, and I had to go to the studio to record. The studio was right around the corner from his house. I told him to stay up because it would only be half an hour, but it turned out to be more like three and a half hours! When I finally called he was half asleep, but I picked him up anyway. It was a hot summer night, so we drove to a secluded park, and I was so shocked he wasn't mad that I took so long. We sat in the car for two hours, talking and looking at the stars until 3:00 A.M.! The next day I wrote "Imagine."

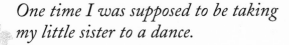

One time I was supposed to be taking my little sister to a dance.

It was one of her first school dances. My mom was sick and my dad wasn't home. One of my best friends and I went to meet my boyfriend and his cousin. We were out looking for limos (for the upcoming prom) and we didn't find any official, nice-looking limos. So we went back to the cousin's house and we were all just chillin'. We were talking and watching TV, a little kissy-kissy here and there (my boyfriend and I weren't at the stage yet to go any further). So we were all just kickin' it and having a good time and we ended up hanging out three or four hours over the time we were supposed to. I remembered I had to take my sister to the dance by 7:00, and it was 8:30! And it took me thirty minutes to get back to my house.

So I got up quickly and looked in the mirror, and I said, "Oh my gosh!" I had this huge black & purple & blue hickey on my neck. And I mean, this is HUGE! So I'm flying home. My friend and I were doing 90 mph all the way back to the house. And I drive up and I say to my friend, "Look, you have to come with me and bring my little sister to the dance!" So I run into my house, and leave the car running. She's in a dress waiting, but I had to run in and get some makeup because of this hickey. So I'm whipping through all of my dresser drawers, trying to find something to cover this up with. I came out five minutes later and told my mom some lame story about being late—I can't remember exactly what. My hair was brushed over the hickey so nobody would see. I got in the car, went to the dance, and my little sister started mingling with her friends, having a good time. My friend and I went to the bathroom. It was an elementary school bathroom, so everything's really small in there. I'm still trying to cover up this hickey and all these little girls are coming in. The hickey was so huge—it practically took up half my neck! But I covered it up well, and my sister had a nice time at the dance. I don't think my mom saw the hickey that night. Maybe she did over the next two days. But I had a really good time that night!

Never Let Go

I always knew it was gonna take a lot
for me to settle down
I've always been the type to play the game
No shame
No strings
Now something in me has changed
I like the way it feels
And when you squeeze me in your arms, oh
I can feel in my soul
I will never ever let you go
And when I lie down at night
and close my eyes
I feel like I'm in heaven for sure
I can see in your smile
you're gonna be around for a while
And when I think about all this time
and love we shared
I know that you ain't
goin' nowhere

Drive Me Crazy

Come with me
I'll show you a good time
I dig your company
So what about tonight?
Forget about everything
Just leave it all behind
Come and ride with me
Everything will be fine

I've been thinking about you, baby
Wondering where you've been
You know you drive me crazy
Make my head spin

When I was a senior in high school, I had a car.

My friend and I would drive up to my boyfriend's college. We used to cut ninth period and go to his school and hang out. He would be missing classes, too. We would walk around the campus and go to the cafeteria. I would just want to be alone with him on the ride back to my house. We would be at my house for two or three hours. Then I would have to go and work out at the gym. His cousin would come and pick him up. And then I couldn't wait to get home from the gym so I could call him up and talk to him! It was crazy.

I remember the phone calls. I would be on the phone with him for hours and hours and hours. I would talk to him for so long that the battery on the portable phone would die. And it would have been fully charged when we started! And then I would call right back on another phone. The only regular phone line we had downstairs was in the kitchen; it was hooked up on a wall over the garbage can. I remember fixing myself a little bed on the floor, so I didn't have to stand up over the garbage. I brought my blankets and pillows there, and I slept kind of on the floor next to the garbage can, *just to talk on the phone!* We would be on the phone for seven or eight hours. It was bananas! There were phenomenal phone bills. It was ridiculous. But when you're in love with someone, you don't see things like that.

No Words

Lately I
don't know why
every time I think about you
I just want to cry

It's not the cry
that makes my heart ache
It's the one that brings me to my knees
and makes me give thanks
that finally I have a chance to breathe
And thank God for all the goodness that He sent me

It's been a while
you've been around
and I think I like how
everything is going now
And spending time
just lets me know
that I need you
and I never want to let you go
And mentally
you were meant for me
Not to mention how I feel
your physicality

So it took a while
but it was worth the wait
It's a different kind of love
when we love make

When I'm sitting with you
Lying with you
Talking with you
I know I love it
when I'm riding with you
Driving with you
Laughing with you
I can't believe I'm so addicted to you
But I'm not ashamed
It's so hard to explain
There are no words
that I could say

My first prom was my boyfriend's junior prom.

I was in ninth grade. I remember wearing a purple dress that I borrowed from my mom, which was too small for her. We were young, and none of my friends were going out with guys who were in our school, so we went with a lot of his friends. It was him and me, his sister, and a guy who was in my grade. Everyone else was so much older than me, and I didn't really know them well. He came up to my house to pick me up in the limo. My mom made everyone get out of the limo and come into my house to take pictures.

I remember going to a club in Manhattan after the prom. There were so many people who smoked! I was the annoying one in the limo who said, "Everyone who's smoking cigarettes, get out and smoke outside!" I couldn't take it. Finally we got to the club. It was official, and they were playing good music. We were really having a good time. I remember one girl who had a little too much to drink, and she collapsed in the club (in the middle of the dance floor) while everyone was partying. Everyone was stepping over her. It was kind of messed up. Her date finally pulled her up.

Tell Me Where I Stand

Tell me where I stand
Are we gonna be hand in hand
Or did I just fall in love with a friend?
Tell me if I'm wrong
We don't have to move it anywhere
I just gotta know where I am

You've gotta know what I feel
when I see your face
It's been a while
we've been dealing with each other this way
And I'm always here
to wipe your tears
Protect and defend
even burden your fears
I am by your side
if they turn on you
I want to be your all
That's what I want to do
I'm giving all I can
But I've gotta know
just where I stand

I always want to see you
smiling back at me
And I've been thinking
this is where I want to be
If I could make it

so you'll never hurt again
I'll do whatever
Say whatever
Give the best I can
Should I have another
waiting on the side?
Should you have a girl
you see at night?
I want to be with you
and this is what I plan
But I got to know
where I stand

One of my friends was telling me about a relationship that she was in. It wasn't anything too serious; they started out just kickin' it and being friends. They were going to the same college. Eventually the feelings started growing, and she was telling me that she didn't know exactly what was going on in the relationship. She knew how she felt, she knew how he felt, but they didn't really talk to each other about it. I guess it was a given, and never really brought up as a topic, that they were a couple. So when it came to dating other people, they were hesitant to discuss that aspect of the relationship. So when I wrote this poem, I had that particular relationship in mind. It's basically about wanting to know where you stand in a relationship. Are we both in this together, or should I stop myself from feeling this way about this guy?

*Once my friend and I were on the way to
my boyfriend's college.*

I was messin' with him, and she was messin' with his cousin.
And she and I were best friends! And the guys were very close.
Anyway, we were on the way to the college. At one point she was
playing a Game Boy, my cell phone was ringing, and my pager was
going off. So I'm listening to my cell phone *and* looking at my
pager at the same time. Neither of us are watching the road, and I
run over these huge boulders in someone's yard. My whole oil pan
underneath my car is scraped out. And I'm just thinking, *This
might be him on the phone, this might be him on the phone!*—not
looking at the road, too interested in whether this is him calling.
And the whole bottom of the oil pan is missing. We get out of the
car and we're like, "Oh man!" But both of us said, "Ah, it's all right.
We'll be able to make it to the school."

So I drove all the way to his college. I mean, the thing was
leaking, and there was smoke coming out of the engine. It was
just ridiculous. But I said, "I don't care—I'm going! We're not
turning back now." No, we drove all the way out there and we
explained to them what happened. He said, "What are you doing?

You shouldn't have come out here with that!" But then we all hopped in the car and went to Wendy's, and then went back to my house. My father was heated. I got it fixed, but the car was never the same.

Watch Me Glisten

He always told me
I looked cute in my shorts
He would watch how I walked
and he would speak out his thoughts
Something told me that I shouldn't be shy
Yeah, he's kind and he's smooth
but he's just another guy
Watch me walk through the sprinkler
so he can see my legs glisten
As the sun hits the drops
there's no way he can miss them
Just as I thought
I got his attention
As he walks in my direction
I perfect my intention

The best advice I've received about love is that you've got to love yourself before others can love you.

But sometimes if you feel that you love that person more than yourself, that's okay. Does that make sense? I guess what I'm trying to say is: love yourself as a person, be happy with yourself and what you do and what you choose, but if you feel so much for someone else that you would give your life for them, that's okay. It's almost like the love you'd receive from your parent—unconditional. For instance with *my* family, I would give my life for my sister, or my mom, or my dad. To feel that you would give your life for someone is very deep. But you have to be respected and treated like you are the most special thing to him on the planet (besides his family—and even that depends on how the family is!).

Constantly

From the first time
I saw your face
You looked into my eyes
and my heart began to race
It felt so real
And yet oh so fake
I never had someone
who could make me feel that way

The way you held me in your arms
Caressing me like I was your charm
Never wanted to let you go
But we had to take it slow
I know it felt so right
Even though it was the first night

You got me into you
The way you moved
The things you do
Constantly on my mind
Thinking about you all the time
You mean so much to me
I see your face in every dream
It's clear so can't you see?
You and I were meant to be

When I wrote "Constantly," I was in a fairly new relationship. We had been dating for about five months, and we were just beginning to experience each other and have fun and enjoy each other's company. It crept up on me how I felt about him. We started off talking on the phone a long time before we started to go out. "From the first time/I saw your face/You looked into my eyes/and my heart began to race" is about how we met at a party. My friend had said to me, "There's this guy I want you to meet and I'm inviting him to my party." She said the same thing to him. It's so funny because he came up to her and said, "Yo, introduce me to that girl over there!" And he didn't realize that I was the girl she was going to introduce him to! So it worked out really well. That's what I had in my heart and in my mind when I wrote "Constantly."

I would have gone to four proms in four years while I was in high school, but on the day of my boyfriend's senior prom (I was a sophomore) along came the drama.

My cousin Shasa and I were out shopping on Jamaica Ave for shoes to match my dress. Our colors were going to be gold and white for this prom. I was going to get my hair and nails done later in the day. Then I got a call that my boyfriend's lungs had collapsed. Oh, it was the worst feeling! I got the call on my cell, and my mom said, "I need you to sit down, Shan, I have something important to tell you." And I was like, "C'mon, Mom! I'm looking for shoes, I have to hurry!" Then she told me and I couldn't believe it. I just wanted to get back home and go to the hospital. It was really bad.

My boyfriend played football, and he had had pneumonia twice. Once we almost lost him. So his lungs were weak from that, but he didn't drink or smoke. So it was a very scary feeling. I remember going to the hospital and inching towards the room because I didn't want to see him feeling bad. He tried to smile and told me to come in, it was okay. I was young and I wasn't feeling ready for this. He had an oxygen mask on and he kept trying to take it off to talk to me. I told him, "Don't do that! You don't have to talk to me." I didn't want him to be worrying about the prom or what we were going to miss. Then I sat home with my mom and cousin that night. He was in the hospital for a few days, but he recovered. The next year he was able to come to *my* junior prom.

Ride Out

It's Friday night
I want to ride out late
and see what's going on
Feeling so right
Going to have a good time
wherever I go
long as I'm having fun
we can stay until the very next day
Sometimes when you're around
you make me want to do wild things

Baby, let's do something crazy
Tell me can you make me
feel like that
Do those things I won't forget

Swerving from lane to lane
Blood rushing through my veins
Looking at me that way
I know what's on your brain
Your hand is slowly moving
up and down my leg
We're almost there
but you act like you can't wait

Baby, let's do something crazy
Tell me can you make me
feel like that
Do those things I won't forget

I wrote "Ride Out" during the summer, and I was thinking about driving fast on a hot summer night in the car from Long Island to Manhattan. I was thinking about being with a guy, and just going out to have a good time. I felt like "party, party, party!" and just very free-spirited. It's Friday night. Nothing to really worry about. Sometimes when you're in the car with a special someone, and it's just the two of you, you're in your own little world. That's where my heart was when I wrote this.

Satisfied

Let me tell you how I like it
If we're all in a crowd
I like to be the one they single out
Let me tell you how to please me
Can you get it crunk and make my body jump?
Do you think you can handle
a girl like me?
If you can take it there you are the man
I want you to be

Let me tell you who makes it hot
Boy, just show me what you got
Time and time I fantasize
I just want to be satisfied

Everybody wants to talk about game
I want to know who can rock it in the fast lane
Everybody wants to brag about things
About the Bentleys, the diamonds, and the platinum rings
Do you think you have a tighter kinda?
Because if you have it then you are the man
I want you to be

Let me tell you who makes it hot
Boy, just show me what you got
Time and time I fantasize
I just want to be satisfied

At my junior prom, my friend had a boyfriend whose uncle owned a limo service.

So we were going to get a discount. We were so excited because we thought a nice limo was coming to get us. Well, that limo looked like it was from 1949! It had an ugly square top, and it was an eggshell color. It had nasty wings in the back that looked like Batman wings. The light switch was a big rope that you pulled down on, like a big bell or something. We were all so embarrassed to pull up at the high school in that nasty, nasty limo. But we all looked cute, and we took a lot of pictures. We danced and ate. We had a good time that night.

Baby Girl

I will always be your baby girl
And I would follow you around the world
Could never care for no one else
If I'm without you, I'm by myself

I will always be your baby girl
And I would follow you around the world
It doesn't matter what we're going through
No matter what, I'm staying here with you

JEALOUSY

Jealousy has definitely affected my previous relationships—in both good and bad ways.

Usually when someone is jealous, it's a sign that they care. In the beginning, it seems like "Oh, it's so sweet—he's mad and stuff!" I'd go out and not say anything to him. He'd get mad, and to me that meant: He cares about what I'm doing and he's thinking about me. It sends a sign, in the beginning, that he wants to be with me.

But jealousy can go both ways. Sometimes it can turn into something that's not really healthy. It can turn into a possessive type of thing. And you don't want that in relationships because that leads to humongous arguments. You start feeling like he owns you, and you have to start answering to him, almost like he's a father figure. I have one dad already! So when I'm in a relationship with a guy, I don't want to be treated like he's my dad.

Insecure

It was six o'clock
when he called my house
he's asking "where was I"
and "did I go out"
I'm trying to figure out
why he's calling me
Trying to question me
while I'm half asleep
So I say "call me back
in the afternoon"
And he says "tell me first
if you're all alone
because I thought I heard
somebody moan"
So then I turned over
and hung up the phone

You should leave him
if he's acting like
he always wants
to fuss and fight
And trying to tell
you about yourself
And always looking
through your cell
And questioning
on where you've been
And always hating
all your friends

And showing that
he's insecure,
by going through
your personal drawer

I don't know why
I end up with those jealous guys
The insecure types
The ones who drive by your house at night
To see if your car is there
To make sure you didn't go anywhere
And tries to justify his actions
by telling you how much he cares

He showed up at my house
at a quarter to
and now he's trying
to bang out my windowsill
So when I did decide
to let him in
he's all up in my face
asking where I've been
So I say "did you really
drive way out here
to run that same ol' same ol'
up in my ear"
Then he says "answer me
before I get mad!"
So then I slammed the door
and went back to bed

Is it me or could it be
a jealous streak caused by insecurity?

The truth is out
I can't be around someone
who's always worrying
if I'm out cheating on him

"Insecure" is basically about what I was going through in my relationship at that particular time. In fact, most of the stuff described in this poem happened during one particular night. But in general, this is just about some of the weird, crazy things you have to deal with when you're in a relationship.

I remember being jealous myself, even if sometimes my boyfriend did call me to tell me he's going out with his friends—you know, to a party or just to hang out.

I would be like, "What? What do you mean you're going out with your friends? You need to be here with me! Forget your friends." And I would do vindictive stuff, like saying, "You're going to go out with your friends? Okay, then I'm just going to find somebody and go out with him." And I would be upset because it felt like he was choosing to hang out with his friends rather than spend time with me at home. Or what if *I* wanted to go out with him that night? So I would do stuff like hang up the phone on him, which would cause a stupid argument. He would call back and say, "Why did you hang up?" and I would say, "Because I'm mad!" It's just really unnecessary, but when you feel passionate about someone, it makes you do crazy things.

Choices

Can you tell me what you said
when you saw her that day?
Did you like the way she smiled?
Did you watch her walk away?
Did it feel like you wanted her
back in your life?
Can you tell me how you feel?
'Cause something just ain't right

If it's me you don't want
I'm gone
I'm out of your life
Just be honest
Let me know what you're feeling inside
Because it's better that you tell me
than run around wild
I'll respect you even more
and we can say our good-byes

Waking up is just not the same
Feeling my life is unraveling
Just doesn't seem to be
working out for me
When I look in your eyes
they don't shine for me
When I pick up the phone
there's no warmth in hello

It's been four months
Seems like ten years, though

We don't go anywhere
We don't have much to share
And I know that your heart
is chasing someone else
Is it all my fault?
Do I blame myself?
She made a mark in your life
Why'd it interfere with mine?
It's a risk that I'll take
but this decision you've got to make

I never thought
this would apply to me
Not knowing if I am the one
who keeps you happy
Although I know I have no control
It seems she has
your heart and soul

Another part of jealousy that's not healthy is when a guy will get upset with his wife or girlfriend because she's wearing a short skirt, or she's wearing a top with her stomach out.

And he'll say, "What are you doing? You can't wear that out!" Even if it's not anything provocative or trashy looking, some men can't take the fact that their woman is beautiful and (in a classy way) wants to show it off. Some guys are like, "Oh no—this is just for me and only me behind closed doors. I don't want anyone to see what I got!"

There have been many occasions when I've witnessed a couple going out, getting ready to get dressed and hop in the car and the guy is like, "Whoa, why do you have this skirt on? Why do you have to wear this? Why can't you have a top where your stomach is covered?" And it just ruins the whole mood, if you're going to the movies or out to eat or to a baby shower or to the mall. It just kills the mood if he's jealous and doesn't want his woman to be seen. On the flip side, if a guy is at a job where he deals with a lot of women, or if his cell phone is constantly ringing but it's business-oriented, sometimes his girlfriend will pick up the phone and say, "What are you doing calling my man? This is my man." And the female would have been calling for business!

One time, some associates and I went to a club. The couple I was with had been together for a long time (they had a child together, too). We pulled up to the club and the female saw one of her man's exes going in. I guess this woman wasn't secure with her appearance, because when she saw the ex she said, "No, we've got to go back to the house so I can get myself together, get myself ready. There's no way that this girl's gonna come and try to steal my man!" I'm not even sure if that was the other woman's intentions. So we had to go *all the way* back to the house so this woman could change. And I was mesmerized! I couldn't believe she was really that insecure. Obviously when you're insecure it leads to jealousy, but this was crazy! After she had dressed up and did her hair over, we went back to the club. The ex was there, minding her own business. No one had done anything to cause a commotion. So we're all in the club, my two associates and I, and my female associate goes over and starts dancing near the ex, and she spills a drink on her— on purpose! (You know, "accidentally on purpose.") And it was ridiculous, because I don't believe the ex even looked his way all night. So jealousy can be an ugly issue. In the beginning it seems so sweet, but then it just gets too possessive. It's not a good thing.

To the Club

I can't help it when a guy is watching me
And I can't help it if he wants to buy a drink
And I'm not mad that you didn't get to come
You see, I can't bring my man to the club

Me and her were going to the club that night
I saw him and I knew that he was just my type
We're rolling through the club
and he blinked his eye
licked his lip real slow
then he said "hello"
He made his way to say "How ya doing? What's your name?"
I told him "I'm Ashanti" and he said "I'm glad you came"
He asked about my man and when's the next time I'll be free
I smiled and shook my head
I said "Thank you for the drink"

I was dancing on the floor because my song was on
He pulled up behind me, said his name was Sean
He told me that he liked
the way I moved my hips
and snapped my fingertips
and then I licked my lips
It was going on three and we decided to leave
He walked me to the car and said he'll pay my parking fee
As we're rolling out the lot he said he wanted to chill
I smiled and shook my head
I said "Thanks for paying the bill!"

I can't help it if I kind of want to flirt
And I can't help it if he's looking up my skirt
And I'm not mad because I'm only having fun
You see, I can't bring my man to the club

Writing this, I was thinking about different situations that have occurred while having a good time on a summer night at the club. Sometimes when a guy is too pushy or aggressive, you have to be nasty and put him in his place. But most of the time when a guy is trying to kick it to me or trying to holler, I just say "Thanks, but no thanks" or "Thanks for the compliment" if I don't want to take it there. You let him down nice and easy so you don't have any confrontations. It's funny how a guy will buy a girl a drink, but sometimes when they buy a drink they expect certain things in return. You just have to say, "Thank you for the drink, but that's about it. I didn't ask you to buy me a drink—I can afford a drink!" Sometimes guys get the wrong idea because some females are down for giving it up for a drink. They kind of ruin it for the women who don't get down like that. As long as you're clear, and not rude, you won't have any problems. So when I wrote this my mind was definitely in the club on a nice hot summer night.

I remember I was at a party—someone's sweet sixteen—and I was dancing with a guy.

The guy that I came with was in the bathroom, and the guy that I was dancing with was like a distant cousin. We were just having a good time on the dance floor. It was a nice party. Anyway, my date came back from the bathroom and saw us dancing and attempted to separate us (you know, with his hands, not in a nice way), but some of the guys around us yoked him up. It created a small commotion. I was like, "What? What is the problem? I'm just dancing." He had this screw face on, and he was all heated and mad. I looked at him and said, "Yo, what are you doing? You're embarrassing me. You can't keep your cool because I'm dancing with another guy, and he's my distant cousin! But even if he wasn't, so what? I was just dancing and it wasn't a big deal." And I remember this ruined the whole night. I was thinking that this was a side of him I hadn't seen.

We went back to his house to hang out, but I was just ready to go home. We were all having such a great night, and he just ruined it, and I didn't feel like hanging with him any more that night. Afterwards, he thought about it, and he said, "I know I shouldn't have done it, but when I saw you dancing and laughing with another guy, it made me feel small." It came out of being jealous.

Misunderstood

I don't know why things change
from the day that I first found you
Why do you act so strange
every time that I'm around you?

Don't want to hurt nobody
Let me tell you how I feel
Just want to have somebody
I can trust
and knows the deal
Don't want to make you mad
Telling you about last night
and how much fun I had
Just because I'm not with you
I don't need your attitude

Baby, I don't need you
but I want you
so I got you
Got you by my side
when things ain't going right
Happy when I see you
but I need to
keep it real with you
No relationships
I'm just trying to live

The other day you asked
why I came home late

and who was I with?
Don't get me wrong
I know you care
But I can't get down with
all that questioning
I like spending time with you
but don't get the wrong idea
Don't make me your priority
Because to settle down now
just ain't me

Baby, I don't need you
but I want you
so I got you
Got you by my side
when things ain't going right
Happy when I see you
but I need to
keep it real with you
No relationships
I'm just trying to live

I wrote "Misunderstood" because I was in a relationship with somebody and we were going through a tough time. We kind of ventured out. I wouldn't say we drifted away from each other, but we just weren't getting along. We were still an item, though. Even if I went out and did something or he went out and did something, we still knew who we loved and who was a priority. In this branch-out (in our relationship) I remember seeing this one guy to kill my boredom, and to get back at my boyfriend. Because my boyfriend and I were just arguing and it was a tough time, so I needed something else to do. Something to get my mind off of it. So I started dealing with this other guy, but it wasn't anything serious at all. I had to let him know that I didn't need him, but I wanted him—I wanted to chill as friends, but don't get the wrong idea about where this is going. We can have fun together and go to the movies, but don't think I'm trying to have a relationship with you.

Jealousy not only interferes with loving relationships (between a boyfriend and a girlfriend), but with relationships between best friends, regular friends, and even enemies!

Jealousy played a major role in a "breakup" I had with a good friend of mine. I had decided to be in a relationship with a guy, and the friend and I had a falling-out over it. It lasted a very long time. I started spending a lot of time with him. I never wanted to shut her out, but I guess she felt that way. Being in a relationship with a friend and then being in a relationship with your man causes conflict sometimes. Either one or the other will sometimes feel like you're not giving them enough attention.

Tunnel Vision

When I stepped in the room
I saw your face
watching me
and every move I made
But the way that you had your arms
around her
I decided to look the other way
It was killing me to think that I
might have found something I like
And there's nothing I could do
because she came here with you

From the first time I saw your face
something told me I'd never be the same
I'm thinking she should be replaced
but I know that's not right,
something's gotta change

As the night went on
I enjoyed the company
of all of the guys
who tried to talk to me
In the back of my mind
I knew there was nothing that excited me
until you passed by

You kind of brushed my shoulder
and I grew a little bit warmer
I remembered you came with her

and I didn't want to offend her
But then you turned around
and grabbed my hand
and I did not let go

Writing this poem, my frame of mind was about not wanting to disrespect someone, another female, even though you have feelings for a guy who doesn't belong to you. He kind of came on to you, and although you knew it was wrong and you knew he had someone else, you kind of followed him. You knew it was wrong, but you didn't know if it was wrong for you to feel that way, so your conscience was playing with you.

One time a friend of mine was dating this guy.

He was slightly older than her, but not by too many years. They were dating for a while, but I didn't think it was anything serious. I really couldn't see it. Then a couple of months later, he started dating her younger sister! I was like, "That is terrible!" I was actually mad at all three of them, because that was just so nasty to me.

Show Me

What did I do wrong
to make you say you wanted
someone else?
It's in the way you act
I can tell
when love is felt
You don't understand
how much your words
stay in my head
And I don't know how
I get vexed
at certain things you've said

And I know you know
you mean so much to me
You've got to let me know
Do you really want me?

I love you
Show me love, too
I really want you around

I don't have time for you
to play with my mind
And I will survive
and move on without you
Don't get me wrong
The love we had was strong

But I can't put myself down for no one, nohow
And I know you know
you mean so much to me
You've got to let me know
Do you really want me?

Overall, jealousy has affected my relationships negatively.

It has brought a lot of arguments, a lot of torment, a lot of heartache. But then after that, it brought a lot of good making up! Because I believe if you're truly in love, then those feelings pass, and you can admit you were wrong. So sometimes, the making up part is *fantastic!* Once in a while it's good to be a bit jealous, but it definitely depends on how you express it. Sometimes arguments that stem from jealousy result in domestic violence, which is serious. Unfortunately, I've witnessed plenty of relationships that were violent, and it's very scary. My heart goes out to the many victims of domestic violence. So jealousy is something you don't want too much of. It's a strain on the relationship, and can later result in turmoil or even be fatal.

BREAKING UP

Everyone's different, but breaking up is always hard.

Depending on what the reason was, you either want to have a nice clean break or remain friends and keep in contact. It's always very hard when one person wants to get out of a relationship and one person wants to stay. Sometimes you just fall out of love, and it's not anything where there's heartache or pain or cheating or lying or arguing or screaming every day. You probably still love the person as a person, but you're not in love with him. It's really hard to get out of relationships where there's really nothing going wrong, you're just falling out of love. I had a breakup where I just didn't want to be in the relationship anymore. But I wanted to remain friends, remain cool, and not have any negativity. It was hard because I knew I was going to hurt him.

On the other hand, when you are dealing with a relationship that does involve arguing and screaming and yelling and "I hate you, you cheated on me!"—that hurts like a ton of bricks when you initially break. But then you just have to keep strong for those first couple of days, and you'll have the breakthrough. It's like a breath of fresh air. You say, "Oh, no more drama! No more stress!" You feel free—you get a taste of that freedom again. It's much easier when you don't have to deal with the arguing anymore. The little bit of love that you felt, the happiness that you shared was definitely not worth all the screams and heartache and pain that happened in the relationship.

Roll the Dice

If you're going
then go ahead and leave
Don't stay if you don't
want to be here with me
With or without you
I'll be good with life
So take a chance
and roll the dice

No matter what I do
there's nothing that's been good for you
No matter what I say
you always got to have your way
It seems like after all this time
you would have known
that you had something hard to find
I'm not easy to come by

I'm not your average type.

Don't think that because I love you, babe,
you're going to sit around threatening me
So if you want to leave
I guess you've got to leave
Please believe me
There are no strings

Day after day it feels like
I'm fighting for something that's gone

Don't see your boots or suits
It seems you've already moved on
I'm tired of hearing you talk the talk
So if you're walking, baby, walk the walk
I told you once, I told you twice
This could be the biggest change of your life
If you're a big man, be a big man
Stop the talkin', roll your dice

At this point I was in a relationship where I was fed up with all the commentary and all the nonsense. If you don't like what's going on and you don't want to be in this relationship, then go ahead and leave. If you don't want to deal with this anymore, then why are you still standing here? Why are you calling me? Make up your mind, stop paddling back and forth like a Ping-Pong ball. That's what I was thinking about when I wrote this.

If a guy is cheating on you, and sometimes your heart aches, but the majority of the time you're happy and you can't find that happiness anywhere else, then there's nothing anyone can do about it.

No matter what the spectators say—the people on the outside of the relationship looking in—if that's what makes you happy and nothing else makes you happy, then maybe that's the ride you need to choose. It's unfortunate (I don't wish that on anyone!), but some people definitely go through that. I would say don't lower your standards or settle, but sometimes you just go for that happiness. You want your heart to beat with joy. If it's going to make you happy, that's what's important.

Walkout

Now it's time for you to see
Gotta pack up your bags and leave
I don't want to hurt no more
Waiting by the door
to see if you would come back to me

I've given you everything
that you've ever needed and more
All you did was take from me
and have your way with me
and to me that's like breaking the law

So I can't stand you no more
Can't love you no more
Can't have you come around oh no more
Won't kiss you no more
Won't miss you no more
Finally gotta see you walkin'
right out my door

A breakup can be something very, very vigorous that goes up and down and up and down.

You feel lonely at night. You feel like going to the movies or just being snuggled up with someone. And you realize you're just not with this guy or girl anymore. The person's just not there. Sometimes you get a little lonely, but that's when you have to tough it out and find a family member to watch that movie with you! That's usually when you cause yourself more torture by thinking of the person. Breaking up is just a very tough thing.

No Excuses

11:30 has come and gone
and still no call from you
Why did you have me waiting here
if you weren't coming through?
I couldn't fall asleep that night
and you came by around 3:00
You said "Baby, I'm sorry, I should
have called. The guys took me out.
It just wasn't my fault."

I don't want to hear any more excuses
Everything you say turns to a lie
I don't want to see your face anymore
So baby good-bye, baby good-bye

Everything I shared with you
took first priority
I don't know why it was so hard
to give that back to me
Now I think I can see
you're never going to change for me
There is nothing to be done
because you're not ready for a woman

There are too many men out there
who want me
for me to sit around and take this
There are too many men out there

to love me
for me to ever have to deal with this
There are too many men out there
to need me
for you to have to be the one I chase
There are too many men out there
who feel me
Already up to come and take your place

This is another episode that went down. It's about feeling like you got stood up. When you and your man have a date with each other, and you're all dressed and ready to go, and you have your perfume on and your hair done, and you're just sitting there staring at the wall (duh!), saying, "All right, what is going on?" He said he was coming. I got dressed. I didn't go out with my girls. I really want to see him. I'm looking forward to being with him and spending time with him. He has the nerve to stand me up! He didn't show up and then he comes back hours later with a lame excuse about how his fellas took him out. And they wouldn't let him go. And this is something that really happened to me—almost exactly! It was 11:30 and I was waiting for his call. He doesn't show up until 3:30, and when he did he had some lame story about his friends taking him out. I didn't even want to see him anymore. It was driving me crazy! There were too many guys out there who I could deal with (who wanted to deal with me) for me to put up with this nonsense. So "No Excuses" is a poem that I experienced—almost exactly as it's written here!

In relationships, you have to love yourself first or else your misery is going to bring misery to the other person.

If you're unhappy, it's gonna make the whole relationship unhappy.

Gotta Get Out

I don't know what's come over me
But I know this is driving me crazy
I don't know if I'm wrong
feeling this way
There is something deep inside
that I can't hide
And I know that I've got to stop
running away
So here is what I'll say

I've got to get out
and learn what life's about
Be sure that you're the one for me
And if so I'll know but now I don't
So let me go and see

We've been together for so long
And I know this is
tearing me apart
To know that I might miss
out on something
I have never gotten to experience

Don't ever think for a moment
that I don't love you
And if you love me
then you'll trust me
And you know that I'm right
so I'm leaving you tonight

I've got to get out
and learn what life's about
Be sure that you're the one for me
And if so I'll know but now I don't
So let me go and see

When I wrote this I was at a point in my relationship where I was really, really in love but I wanted to make sure that I was in love 100%, because I was dealing with so much with him and he was dealing with so much with me. I wanted to test it. I wanted to see if I could feel this much for someone else, and if I could, then he and I didn't have true love. So this was basically about trying to get out of a relationship and experience a little bit more, because we were very young. And we were into a monogamous relationship, and it was turning into something really serious. People around knew it was a committed relationship. So I wanted to make sure that if I was going to be committed to something, that it was real and true and "the one." We were both so young and the relationship was young, so I wanted to make sure that this was it. So this came out of something that was very heartfelt. Before you marry someone, you want to make sure he or she is the right person.

Sometimes a breakup can be something very dangerous.

When someone's obsessed or infatuated with you, it can be very dangerous to rip away from them. You can have a stalker—a person who just doesn't want to let go, who just can't leave you alone. He or she just shows up out of nowhere. It's very selfish. He or she would rather you suffer and be in his or her life than let you pursue your own happiness. So, some breakups are scary and dangerous.

On My Own

When I woke up this morning
I said "I know I deserve much better"
Sitting around
Waiting around
For you to try to get it right
So many times I tried to tell myself
"It's all a phase"
Everywhere I would go they'd see the pain
all on my face

Everybody always asking
why I stayed
Believing that somehow you'd learn
to change your ways
But I would make up an excuse
about better days
Knowing that I should have turned
and walked away
Staring at memories of yesterday
thinking 'bout all the games
you used to play
I don't know why you're trying to come back now
It's funny how things come back around

Where were you when I was all alone?
See, I don't need you now
I'm standing on my own
And I don't know why you're trying
to come back now

When I was down, you weren't around
So go

Now after all this time
you finally realized that I'm over you
because I'm not there for you
the way you're used to
Eventually I knew you'd come back
begging on your knees
I turned my back on you today
and here is what I'll say

Where were you when I was all alone?
See, I don't need you now
I'm standing on my own
And I don't know why you're trying
to come back now
When I was down, you weren't around
So go

This is about feeling that every single day is the same thing. There's nothing on the planet that's good enough. There's nothing that can prevent these arguments that we're having. I was kind of miserable when I wrote this, and I was tired of people asking what's going on and how I'm doing, because they could see I wasn't right. They could see that I didn't feel good. My relationship at the time was just crazy, and it was about time that I straightened up. I had to stop settling and stop dealing with all the nonsense. When I felt kind of alone or down, my boyfriend was never there to cheer me up. We'd have these arguments, but when you really love someone, there's supposed to be some love shown after the argument. There is such a thing as unconditional love. What I wanted to demonstrate in the poem was that this guy wasn't there for his girlfriend. She was alone, feeling bad and down after these arguments. So it really proved that he didn't care much about her. This is very similar to what I went through at that time. In the poem, he really does leave, but she gets her strength and she gets over him and she throws it back in his face. She says, "You know what? You weren't here when I needed you, so POOF! I'm out. I'm gonna stand on my own."

There are so many bad things that guys do.

For one thing, they manipulate and they lie. And they try to make something seem like one thing when it's really not that. That really takes the cake for me! Just be up-front and everything will be okay. If you're not looking for a monogamous relationship—just say it! Sometimes they try to get what they want by lying and deceiving. And sometimes women are just as bad. They'll use a guy's emotions to get to his pockets, or they just won't be honest. I just feel it's a win/win situation with honesty. They say the truth hurts, but hey, it beats not knowing.

Us

Woke up about 4:00 A.M., you see
Found out you weren't lyin' here next to me
I called your friend
You weren't in—where could he be?
Let me tell you how Kevin broke it down to me
He saw ya Benz, it was parked on Tenth Street
Now I'm realizin' who you went to meet
Was it love or was it lust?
Gave you all my trust
but did you think about us?

When you went out last night
Kissed me good-bye, then you went to find her
That's all right 'cause your game ain't tight
Found out all your lies

I won't be your fool
Now there's nothing you can say or do
You can go your way and I will go mine
Be careful who you call your friends
'Cause your boy's no good
He was trying to get in
when he caught you slippin'
but that's all right
You are out of my life

I've seen guys do terrible things to friends of mine.

I remember my girls and I were getting things together for the senior prom: the money for the tickets, the money for the limo and dinner, etc. We were just getting the whole prom package together, and we were a couple of weeks ahead in what we had to do. I remember during our lunch period in school we would drive out to Westbury, to my friend's boyfriend's job, so she could see him and talk to him on his lunch break. One time we were going up there to collect his share of the prom money. But it seemed like each and every time we went up there he would have another excuse as to why he didn't have the money! So I said, "Okay, he's playing games now, you better put him in check. I don't know what's going on, but it looks like he's being a bit deceiving with this whole money-giving thing." My friend finally puts in the money that he's supposed to put in, but we would still go out there to make sure that he was on point with what was going on. Everything was cool, even though sometimes this guy acted stupid.

So, day of the prom comes around. Our prom was held in the city—even though we're on Long Island—so we had to get ready fairly early to head out there. My cousin Shasa was putting on my makeup, and I got into this custom-made dress that was just bananas. I was getting a bit nervous because my boyfriend was running late. He was coming from Queens, and I was in Glen Cove, Long Island. The traffic on the Long Island Expressway is just disgusting. He was late, and I was getting mad at him: "This is my damn prom—you're late for everything!" So I'm heated. He finally comes up to my house and the limo comes almost simultaneously to pick us up. We get in the limo and drive to my friend's house. When we pull up in front of her house, she's outside—without her boyfriend! We asked where he was, and the look on her face was one I'll never forget. She looked sad, humiliated, devastated, angry, and just shocked all at the same time. She said, "I don't know where he is. I've been calling him, he ain't calling me back. Nobody knows where he is. He didn't show up, so I don't know what's going on." I said, "WHAT!? You've got to be kidding me!" It was the worst. I can't even say the words I want to use to describe how I felt about this guy! So she ended up going with my ex-boyfriend's best friend, who was a good friend of hers. It was cool, but it was also kind of awkward. To find out that her man isn't coming, and then she's going with my ex's best friend . . . it was kind of crazy. A couple of weeks later the guy called and apologized. Something lame about how he didn't know how to say he didn't want to go. He was a bit older than her—nineteen or twenty—and he couldn't open up his mouth to say he didn't want to go?

And the weird thing was, that wasn't the only friend of mine who was stood up that night! After the earlier drama, we went to pick up my other friend and the same thing happened to her. (And to think I was mad at my boyfriend earlier for being late, then nobody else's boyfriend showed up!) This friend's date was at her house that day, earlier in the afternoon, but come prom time she couldn't find him. And then she wasn't going to go, but we told her to—her date was a dummy anyway. She ended up going with my boyfriend's best friend. That is so crazy! Crazy! She ended up going with my boyfriend's best friend, because they had to drop him off and he happened to be in the car. She didn't even know him. I would have to say that was one of the lowest things I've seen guys do. To stand someone up on prom night—with no excuse, no explanation, not an emergency, nothing! That was horrible.

Three-Way

There's been something on my mind
I want to let it out today
I heard that you've been conversatin'
with this girl from around my way
Now I'm not jumping to conclusions
I just want to know the deal
Yes, I trust you
but I want to know
if you can keep it real

I've been waiting for the day
when it would finally come to light
I've been thinking you've been cheatin'
and you know that's just not right!
So just to be sure
I gave you a call
to see exactly what you'd say
You said, *"Girl, you know I'm not lying!"*
Good, let's call her on three-way

Now stay on the line
We've gotta end this today
When she picks up the phone
Talk like nothing's wrong

Now I've got you on three-way

I'm a really strong person.

I'm not your average gullible Susie. I don't chase a guy, and I try not to let him know if he's hurting me. One piece of advice I give my friends is play hard to get! Guys like a challenge. If a guy is attracted to you—the way you dress, carry yourself, do your hair, your personality, whatever—they like a challenge. Don't be so easy! Because once they learn that they can get you and do whatever they want, then they're like, "Okay, I don't have to work hard or respect her, because I know I can get whatever. She's gullible."

Don't call him every day. And sometimes when he calls you, don't call him back. Don't let him think that he's on your mind like that! Let him sweat it out a little bit. I used to tell people not to lend their things out to guys. I remember my friend lent a guy her Walkman, and he never gave it back. And she didn't make him buy her a new one. They weren't dating, but she really, really liked him. And she would call him all the time. He just wasn't showing as much interest. So I said to her, "I know you like him, but let him sweat you a little bit. Don't give in."

As far as sex is concerned, I would always tell my friends, "Don't give in so easily!" From my parents I picked up some very positive traits. I'm an old soul. And my friends were just not up on things that seemed like common sense to me. I would say, "Don't sleep with this guy! He's not worth it. You're too special for that." If he's not willing to hang out with you instead of his friends, then what are you doing? Make him wait, make him sweat you. Make him think, "She must be the bomb, she's not giving in to me!" Guys like to feel like they've accomplished something, that they've worked hard at getting you. That's what makes you special.

Also, don't depend solely on a guy for all of your comfort or all of your love. Don't let a guy be the center of your happiness. Even if you feel like your family and friends are not being supportive of you, and this certain guy is, don't put all of your eggs in one basket. It's good to have a backup plan, so don't limit yourself. You've got to give it up, suck it up, and keep it moving.

HOPE

My perfect date would be on a tropical island!

Give me about 80 degrees of warm sun and a beach. Bright blue skies, and warm, tropical blue water. We'd start out by going to a restaurant for a big breakfast with tropical drinks and tropical music. Then we'd go to a comedy club, and we'd laugh and enjoy each other's company as we sat in the theater. Then we'd go out on a boat ride (not too far out in the sea, though!), and have a great lunch with Caribbean food. Then we'd lie out on the beach and get tan, and later go out for a night of Caribbean music and dancing at one of the hottest clubs. Of course we'd go back to the beach and sit in the sand, and just love each other. Finally we'd head back to the illest hotel with a water bed, huge flat-screen television, and end the night as one.

Move

Ever since I saw you watching me
you made me think I had to play it smooth
and let you make your move

So I paid little attention
and I tried not to mention
how fine you were to me
Even if you kinda knew
this is what you should do

Make your move
and make it right
And don't be shy
What about tonight?
The stars are bright
The night is young
Let's get together
and have some fun

My hopes and dreams for the future regarding love is to have someone who truly loves me.

Not for my music, not for the money, not for the status. Just to have someone who is honestly in love with who I am. Someone who respects me, who appreciates me for me. Someone who doesn't try to change me or mold me into someone else. I want to find someone who is my friend more than anything else, and who is trustworthy. I want to share great chemistry and companionship, and just have the type of relationship where I don't have to change. I want to hate him, and love him, and grow, and mature, and experience life together, and experience each other together. I want to go through good times and bad times with this person. I want to be able to share each and every thing with him, and tell him all the things I don't like about myself and all the things I love about myself. And just let that be okay. I want to hurt when he's gone, and I want to have him with me for whatever it is I'm doing. I don't want to have to hide anything. I definitely want him to be spiritual. I'm not saying he has to go to church every single Sunday, but he has to be spiritual and he has to come with me for the most part. I want to have excitement and romance. I want the part in his heart and in his life that no one can ever fill, and I want him to feel the same way. I want to grow old with him, and watch our kids grow. I want to be head-over-heels in love, and enjoy life. I just pray that I'll have a strong relationship. I want genuine happiness, health, and a family.

Love Discovered

Can you be my dream come true?
It's been a long time that I've been
waiting for you
I never wanted to care
Now I've found someone
who I want to be my Teddy Bear
So I can squeeze you when I want
and you can hold me all night long
You're everything I want
You're everything I need
But you can't take advantage of me

I want to run away with you
I have to know if you feel the way I do
Ever since that day in June
Your first kiss left me speechless
I want to know if this is right
and I know I'll never have to fight
You're everything I want
You're everything I need
But don't take advantage of me

I want to be your rose in a glass
Treat me like a princess
I want to be your rose in a glass
Don't break me into pieces

Afterword

In the end, there is one kind of love that endures forever no matter what, and that's the love of family. I am grateful that I have such a large, loving family behind me: My mother, Tina, my father, Kincaid, and my sister, Shia, as well as several cousins, aunts, and uncles who I'm extremely close to. They have definitely been my backbone throughout my struggles and successes. To imagine me here without them would just honestly not make sense.

While growing up I was fortunate enough to have the love of my grandparents, James Davis and Yvonne Myers, may they rest in peace. And still with me, Floretha Douglas, who has been a total influence and inspiration, and has definitely helped shape and mold my life.

When feeling like the world is against you and everything is going wrong, or feeling ashamed, lost, lonely, and confused, to know that you have a family that loves and cares about you and your well-being is by far one of the most precious gifts anyone could ask for. True unconditional love is unparalleled.

Pro Line Studios